Albania

Everything You Need to Know

Copyright © 2024 by Noah Gil-Smith.

All rights reserved. No part of this book may be reproduced, distributed, or transmitted in any form or by any means, including photocopying, recording, or other electronic or mechanical methods, without the prior written permission of the publisher, except in the case of brief quotations embodied in critical reviews and certain other noncommercial uses permitted by copyright law. This book was created with the assistance of Artificial Intelligence. The content presented in this book is for entertainment purposes only. It should not be considered as a substitute for professional advice or comprehensive research. Readers are encouraged to independently verify any information and consult relevant experts for specific matters. The author and publisher disclaim any liability or responsibility for any loss, injury, or inconvenience caused or alleged to be caused directly or indirectly by the information presented in this book.

Introduction to Albania 6

Unveiling Albania's Ancient History 8

The Rise and Fall of Illyrian Civilization 11

Albania: From Roman Conquest to Byzantine Influence. 14

Ottoman Rule: Shaping Albania's Identity 17

Albania in the Modern Era: Independence and Beyond 20

Exploring Albania's Natural Beauty 23

Wildlife Wonders: Flora and Fauna of Albania 25

Albanian Cuisine: A Culinary Journey 27

Delving into Albanian Traditional Dishes 30

Iconic Landmarks: Must-See Tourist Sights in Albania 32

UNESCO World Heritage Sites of Albania 35

Tirana: The Vibrant Capital City 37

Shkodër: Gateway to the North 39

Exploring the Historic Streets of Gjirokastër 41

Berat: City of a Thousand Windows 43

Durres: Where History Meets the Sea. 45

Vlorë: A Coastal Gem with Rich History 47

Korçë: Cultural Capital of Albania 49

Krujë: Home of Albania's National Hero 51

Albanian Festivals and Traditions 53

Folk Music and Dance: Cultural Expressions of Albania 55

Albanian Art and Craftsmanship Through the Ages 57

The Impact of Religion on Albanian Culture 59

Albanian Hospitality: A Warm Welcome Awaits 61

Understanding Albanian Social Etiquette 63

Family Life and Values in Albania 65

Education System in Albania: Past and Present 68

Exploring the Rich Literary Heritage of Albania 71

The Resilience of Albanian Language and Alphabet 73

Glimpses into Albanian Folklore and Mythology 75

Albanian Diaspora: Keeping Traditions Alive Abroad 77

The Albanian Revival: National Awakening in the 19th Century 80

World War II and Albania's Role in the Resistance 83

Albania in the Cold War Era: Isolation and Transition 86

Albania's Journey to European Integration 88

Environmental Challenges and Conservation Efforts 91

Albanian Economy: Opportunities and Challenges 94

Healthcare System in Albania: Past and Present 97

Transportation Infrastructure in Albania 100

Sports and Recreation in Albania 103

Prospects and Challenges for Albania in the 21st Century 106

Epilogue 110

Introduction to Albania

Welcome to the gateway of the Balkans, Albania. Nestled in Southeast Europe, Albania is a land of captivating beauty, rich history, and vibrant culture. Bordered by Montenegro to the northwest, Kosovo to the northeast, North Macedonia to the east, and Greece to the south, Albania boasts a stunning coastline along the Adriatic and Ionian Seas to the west.

With a population of over 2.8 million people, Albania is a diverse tapestry of ethnicities, languages, and traditions. Its capital, Tirana, is a bustling metropolis that perfectly encapsulates the country's blend of ancient heritage and modern dynamism.

The history of Albania is as diverse as its landscape. From the ancient Illyrians to Roman conquests, Byzantine rule to Ottoman occupation, Albania has been shaped by a myriad of civilizations throughout the ages. The struggle for independence in the early 20th century marks a significant chapter in Albania's history, paving the way for the establishment of a sovereign nation.

Albania's natural beauty is awe-inspiring. From the rugged peaks of the Albanian Alps to the pristine beaches of the Riviera, this small country packs a punch when it comes to scenic wonders. The diverse ecosystems support a rich array of flora and fauna, making Albania a paradise for nature lovers and outdoor enthusiasts alike.

But Albania is not just about its landscapes; it's also about its people and their vibrant culture. Albanians are known for their warmth and hospitality, welcoming visitors with open arms and treating them like family. Traditional music and dance are integral parts of Albanian culture, reflecting the country's unique heritage and identity.

The cuisine of Albania is a delightful fusion of Mediterranean and Balkan flavors, featuring fresh seafood, hearty meats, and an abundance of locally grown produce. From savory burek to mouthwatering tave kosi, Albanian cuisine is sure to tantalize your taste buds and leave you craving for more.

Throughout this book, we will delve deeper into the many facets of Albania, exploring its history, culture, cuisine, and natural wonders. Join us on this journey as we uncover the secrets of this enchanting land and discover why Albania truly is a hidden gem waiting to be explored.

Unveiling Albania's Ancient History

Step back in time and journey with us as we unveil the ancient history of Albania, a land steeped in mystery and legend. From the dawn of civilization, the region now known as Albania has been inhabited by various tribes and peoples, each leaving their mark on the land.

One of the earliest inhabitants of Albania were the Illyrians, a tribal confederation who settled in the western Balkans around the 7th century BCE. The Illyrians were known for their warrior culture and decentralized political structure, with numerous tribes scattered across the rugged terrain of present-day Albania.

The Illyrians thrived in a landscape characterized by dense forests, fertile plains, and strategic mountain passes, making them formidable adversaries to their neighbors. They were skilled craftsmen, producing intricate pottery, metalwork, and jewelry that reflected their cultural sophistication.

During the 4th century BCE, the Illyrians came into contact with the expanding Greek and Roman civilizations, leading to a period of cultural exchange and conflict. The coastal city of Epidamnos (modern-day Durrës) became a vital trading hub, linking the Illyrians with merchants from Greece and beyond.

In 229 BCE, the Illyrian king Agron established a powerful kingdom that encompassed much of present-day Albania and parts of neighboring territories. Under Agron's rule, Illyria experienced a period of relative stability and prosperity, with trade flourishing and urban centers developing along the coastline.

However, the rise of Rome posed a significant threat to Illyrian autonomy. In 168 BCE, the Roman Republic launched a series of military campaigns against Illyria, culminating in the defeat of the Illyrian queen Teuta and the annexation of much of Illyrian territory.

Following the Roman conquest, Albania became an integral part of the Roman Empire, with cities such as Dyrrachium (modern-day Durrës) and Apollonia (near modern-day Fier) flourishing as centers of trade and culture. The Romans introduced new architectural styles, infrastructure, and legal institutions to the region, leaving a lasting impact on Albanian society.

The decline of the Roman Empire in the 4th century CE ushered in a period of instability and invasions, as successive waves of barbarian tribes swept through the Balkans. Albania became a battleground for various competing powers, including the Byzantine Empire, the Bulgarian Empire, and the Serbian Kingdom.

By the 11th century, Albania emerged as a distinct political entity, with local chieftains and feudal lords vying for control over the fragmented territory. The arrival of the Byzantine Empire brought Christianity to Albania, laying the foundations for the country's religious and cultural identity.

As we peel back the layers of time, we uncover the rich tapestry of Albania's ancient history, a story of resilience, conquest, and cultural exchange that continues to shape the identity of this enigmatic land. Join us as we delve deeper into the mysteries of Albania's past and unlock the secrets of its ancient civilizations.

The Rise and Fall of Illyrian Civilization

In the annals of ancient history, the Illyrians stand as a testament to the resilience and complexity of the peoples who inhabited the western Balkans. The origins of the Illyrians can be traced back to the early Iron Age, around the 7th century BCE, when various tribal groups began to settle in the rugged terrain of present-day Albania and its surrounding regions.

The Illyrians were a diverse confederation of tribes, each with its own distinct culture, language, and customs. They inhabited a vast territory that stretched from the Adriatic coast to the Danube River, encompassing parts of modern-day Albania, Montenegro, Kosovo, and beyond. Despite their decentralized political structure, the Illyrians shared a common language and cultural heritage, which bound them together as a cohesive ethnic group.

The Illyrians were known for their warrior culture and formidable military prowess. They were skilled horsemen and fierce fighters, capable of resisting external threats and defending their territory with tenacity. Their strategic location in the western Balkans, with its natural barriers of mountains and rivers, made them a formidable adversary to their neighbors.

One of the most famous Illyrian leaders was Queen Teuta, who ruled in the 3rd century BCE. Teuta was known for her daring naval expeditions and aggressive expansionist policies, which brought her into conflict with the growing power of the Roman Republic. The Roman historian Livy chronicled the exploits of Teuta and her encounters with Roman envoys, portraying her as a formidable and fearless leader.

Despite their military prowess, the Illyrians were ultimately unable to withstand the might of Rome. In 168 BCE, the Roman Republic launched a series of military campaigns against Illyria, culminating in the defeat of Queen Teuta and the annexation of much of Illyrian territory. The Illyrians were gradually assimilated into the Roman Empire, adopting Roman customs, language, and legal institutions.

The decline of Illyrian civilization coincided with the rise of Rome as a dominant power in the Mediterranean. As the Roman Empire expanded its reach into the Balkans, Illyria became a strategic province, serving as a vital link between Rome and the eastern territories. The cities of Dyrrachium (modern-day Durrës) and Apollonia (near modern-day Fier) flourished as centers of trade and commerce, benefiting from their proximity to the Adriatic Sea and the lucrative trade routes that crisscrossed the region.

The legacy of the Illyrians lives on in the cultural and linguistic heritage of the modern-day Albanian people. Despite the passage of millennia, traces of Illyrian civilization can still be found in the traditions, customs, and folklore of Albania and its neighboring countries. As we reflect on the rise and fall of Illyrian civilization, we gain a deeper appreciation for the rich tapestry of history that has shaped the land we know today as Albania.

Albania: From Roman Conquest to Byzantine Influence.

Embark with us on a journey through the tumultuous period of Albania's history, from the Roman conquest to the influence of the Byzantine Empire. Following the defeat of the Illyrians by the Roman Republic in 168 BCE, Albania became an integral part of the vast Roman Empire. The Romans brought with them a new era of governance, infrastructure, and culture, transforming the landscape of Albania and leaving a lasting imprint on its society.

During the Roman period, Albania flourished as a strategic province within the empire. Cities such as Dyrrachium (modern-day Durrës) and Apollonia (near modern-day Fier) became important centers of trade and commerce, benefiting from their strategic location along the Adriatic coast. The Romans introduced new architectural styles, including amphitheaters, aqueducts, and roads, which helped to connect Albania with the wider empire and facilitate trade and communication.

Albania's position on the eastern edge of the Roman Empire made it vulnerable to incursions from barbarian tribes and rival powers. In the 4th century CE, the Roman Empire underwent a period of decline and fragmentation, leading to increased instability and insecurity in Albania and its neighboring regions. The rise of Christianity during this period brought about significant changes in Albanian society, as the region gradually converted to the new faith and established ties with the emerging Christian communities of the Byzantine Empire.

By the 6th century CE, Albania had come under the influence of the Byzantine Empire, which succeeded the Eastern Roman Empire following the fall of Rome in 476 CE. The Byzantines brought with them a new era of cultural and religious influence, as Albania became increasingly integrated into the Byzantine sphere of influence. The spread of Orthodox Christianity and the establishment of ecclesiastical structures helped to solidify Byzantine control over the region and shape the religious identity of the Albanian people.

Despite the Byzantine influence, Albania remained a contested territory, subject to invasions and incursions from various powers in the region. In the 11th century, the Normans launched a series of campaigns against the Byzantine Empire, leading to the temporary occupation of parts of Albania. However, Byzantine rule was eventually restored, and Albania remained under Byzantine control until the arrival of the Ottoman Turks in the 15th century.

As we reflect on the period from Roman conquest to Byzantine influence, we gain a deeper understanding of the complex forces and dynamics that shaped the history of Albania. Join us as we continue our exploration of this fascinating land and uncover the mysteries of its past.

Ottoman Rule: Shaping Albania's Identity

Step into the tumultuous era of Ottoman rule, a period that profoundly shaped the identity of Albania. Beginning in the 15th century, Albania fell under the control of the mighty Ottoman Empire, marking the start of a centuries-long period of domination and influence.

The Ottoman conquest of Albania brought significant changes to the region, both culturally and politically. The Albanian people found themselves living within the vast and diverse Ottoman Empire, alongside peoples of various ethnicities, religions, and backgrounds. Under Ottoman rule, Albania became part of a larger imperial framework, with the Sultan in Istanbul exercising authority over local governors and administrators.

The Ottoman Empire was known for its policy of religious tolerance, allowing different faith communities to coexist within its borders. In Albania, this led to a diverse religious landscape, with Muslims, Christians, and Jews living side by side. Despite this tolerance, however, the Ottomans favored Islam as the dominant religion, and many Albanians converted to Islam over the centuries, particularly during the 17th and 18th centuries.

One of the most enduring legacies of Ottoman rule in Albania is the influence of Islamic culture and traditions. Mosques, madrasas, and other Islamic institutions were established throughout the region, contributing to the spread of Islamic knowledge and practice. Islamic architecture, characterized by domes, minarets, and intricate geometric designs, became a defining feature of Albania's urban landscape.

Ottoman rule also had a profound impact on Albanian society and governance. The Ottomans implemented a system of local administration known as the timar system, where land was granted to military officers and administrators in exchange for military service or tax revenue. This system created a class of landowning elites who wielded significant influence over local affairs.

Despite the benefits of Ottoman rule, Albania experienced periods of resistance and rebellion against Ottoman authority. The Albanian people fiercely defended their autonomy and cultural identity, leading to numerous uprisings and revolts throughout the centuries. One of the most notable rebellions was led by the national hero Skanderbeg in the 15th century, who successfully resisted Ottoman rule for over two decades before his eventual defeat.

The decline of the Ottoman Empire in the 19th century brought about significant changes in Albania and the wider Balkans. As Ottoman power waned, nationalist movements emerged, seeking to assert Albanian identity and autonomy. The Albanian National Awakening, known as the Rilindja, saw a resurgence of Albanian language, literature, and culture, laying the foundations for the modern Albanian state.

Albania in the Modern Era: Independence and Beyond

Enter the modern era of Albania, a period marked by struggle, resilience, and transformation. In the late 19th and early 20th centuries, Albania emerged from centuries of Ottoman rule to assert its independence and forge a new path forward. The Albanian National Awakening, known as the Rilindja, played a pivotal role in shaping the country's identity and aspirations for self-determination.

On November 28, 1912, Albania declared its independence from the Ottoman Empire, marking the birth of a sovereign nation. However, the road to independence was fraught with challenges, as Albania faced internal divisions and external threats from neighboring powers. The Treaty of London in 1913 recognized Albania as an independent state, but its borders remained contested, leading to further instability and conflict.

In the aftermath of World War I, Albania experienced a period of political turmoil and instability, as rival factions vied for power and influence. The interwar years saw the rise of authoritarian regimes and the erosion of democratic institutions, as Albania struggled to find its footing as a modern nation-state.

During World War II, Albania was occupied by Italian and then German forces, further exacerbating the country's political and social upheaval. The Albanian resistance movement, led by figures such as Enver Hoxha and Mehmet Shehu, played a crucial role in opposing the fascist occupiers and defending Albanian sovereignty.

Following the end of World War II, Albania underwent a radical transformation under the leadership of Enver Hoxha and the Communist Party of Albania. Hoxha's regime implemented a policy of isolationism and self-reliance, breaking ties with the Soviet Union and pursuing a path of Marxist-Leninist socialism. The regime implemented collectivization and industrialization programs, but also suppressed political dissent and human rights, leading to widespread hardship and repression.

The collapse of communism in Eastern Europe in the late 1980s and early 1990s brought about significant changes in Albania. In 1991, Albania held its first multiparty elections in nearly half a century, marking the end of communist rule and the beginning of a new era of democracy and political pluralism. However, the transition to democracy was not without its challenges, as Albania struggled to overcome the legacy of decades of communist rule and build democratic institutions.

In the decades since the fall of communism, Albania has made significant strides in political and economic development. The country has embraced market reforms and pursued closer integration with Europe, seeking membership in the European Union and NATO. Despite these achievements, Albania continues to face challenges such as corruption, organized crime, and social inequality, as it strives to build a more prosperous and democratic future for its citizens.

Exploring Albania's Natural Beauty

Let's start our journey in the Albanian Alps, a majestic mountain range that stretches across the northern part of the country. Here, you'll find towering peaks, deep valleys, and crystal-clear rivers, making it a paradise for hikers, climbers, and outdoor enthusiasts. The Valbona Valley National Park and Theth National Park are popular destinations for trekking, offering stunning vistas and opportunities to experience traditional Albanian hospitality in mountain guesthouses.

As we travel southward, we encounter the pristine shores of the Albanian Riviera, a hidden gem along the Ionian Sea. With its secluded coves, turquoise waters, and white sandy beaches, the Riviera is a haven for sun-seekers and beachgoers looking to escape the crowds of more popular Mediterranean destinations. The towns of Himara, Saranda, and Dhermi are perfect bases for exploring the coastline and discovering hidden gems like the Blue Eye Spring and the Llogara Pass.

Inland, Albania boasts lush forests, tranquil lakes, and winding rivers that offer opportunities for relaxation and exploration. The Divjaka-Karavasta National Park, home to the largest lagoon in Albania, is a haven for birdwatchers and nature lovers, with over 250 species of birds and diverse ecosystems to discover. The Osumi Canyon, carved by the Osum River over millions of years, offers breathtaking views and opportunities for hiking, rafting, and canyoning.

For those seeking adventure, Albania offers a variety of outdoor activities, from paragliding over the coastal cliffs to caving in the limestone caves of the Vjosë-Nartë Protected Landscape. The country's rugged terrain and pristine wilderness make it an ideal destination for ecotourism and sustainable travel, with initiatives like the Peaks of the Balkans Trail promoting responsible tourism and community development in rural areas.

But Albania's natural beauty is not limited to its landscapes; it also extends beneath the surface of the sea. The waters surrounding Albania are home to a rich variety of marine life, including dolphins, seals, and rare species of fish. Scuba diving and snorkeling enthusiasts can explore underwater caves, coral reefs, and shipwrecks, discovering a hidden world of beauty and wonder beneath the waves.

As we conclude our exploration of Albania's natural beauty, we are reminded of the country's unique and diverse landscapes, which offer something for everyone to enjoy. Whether you're seeking adventure, relaxation, or simply a chance to connect with nature, Albania has it all, waiting to be discovered and explored.

Wildlife Wonders: Flora and Fauna of Albania

Albania's varied geography, which includes mountains, forests, wetlands, and coastline, provides habitats for a remarkable diversity of species, making it a haven for wildlife enthusiasts and nature lovers.

Let's start with Albania's forests, which cover approximately 36% of the country's land area. These forests are home to a variety of tree species, including beech, oak, pine, and fir, as well as rare and endemic plants such as the Macedonian pine and the Albanian lily. The forests provide important habitats for wildlife, including brown bears, wolves, lynxes, and wild boars, as well as numerous species of birds, reptiles, and insects.

Moving to the mountains, the Albanian Alps and other mountain ranges are home to species adapted to high altitudes, such as chamois, ibex, and golden eagles. Alpine meadows are carpeted with wildflowers during the spring and summer months, attracting pollinators like butterflies and bees. In the remote and rugged terrain of the mountains, elusive species like the Balkan lynx and the Eurasian otter find refuge, making these areas important conservation priorities.

Albania's wetlands are also teeming with life, providing vital habitat for migratory birds, amphibians, and aquatic species. The Karavasta Lagoon, located on the central Albanian coast, is the largest lagoon in the country and an important breeding ground for waterfowl such as flamingos, pelicans, and herons. Other wetland areas, such as the Prespa Lakes and the Vjosa River Delta, are also biodiversity hotspots, supporting a wide variety of plant and animal species.

Along the coastline, the Adriatic and Ionian Seas are home to a rich diversity of marine life, including dolphins, seals, and sea turtles. The waters surrounding Albania are also important feeding grounds for migratory species such as tuna, swordfish, and dolphins. Coral reefs and seagrass beds provide important habitat for fish and other marine organisms, while underwater caves and rocky outcrops are home to a variety of invertebrates and crustaceans.

Despite its relatively small size, Albania boasts an impressive number of protected areas, including national parks, nature reserves, and protected landscapes. These areas play a crucial role in conserving Albania's biodiversity and providing refuge for threatened and endangered species. Initiatives such as the Albanian National Agency for Protected Areas work to manage and conserve these areas, ensuring that future generations can continue to enjoy Albania's natural wonders.

Albanian Cuisine: A Culinary Journey

Embark on a culinary journey through the rich and flavorful world of Albanian cuisine, where tradition meets innovation in a tapestry of taste sensations. Albanian food is a reflection of the country's diverse cultural influences, blending Mediterranean flavors with Balkan and Ottoman influences to create dishes that are both comforting and distinctive.

Central to Albanian cuisine is the use of fresh, locally sourced ingredients, including seasonal fruits and vegetables, herbs, dairy products, and meats. With its mild climate and fertile soil, Albania boasts an abundance of produce, from juicy tomatoes and crisp cucumbers to fragrant herbs like oregano, mint, and thyme.

Meat plays a prominent role in Albanian cuisine, with lamb, beef, and poultry featuring prominently in many dishes. One of the most beloved Albanian dishes is qofte, or meatballs, which are typically made with minced meat, onions, and spices, then grilled or fried to perfection. Another popular meat dish is tavë kosi, a baked casserole made with tender lamb or beef, rice, and yogurt, flavored with garlic and herbs.

Seafood also holds a special place in Albanian cuisine, thanks to the country's long coastline along the Adriatic and Ionian Seas. Fresh fish and shellfish are often grilled, fried, or stewed and served with lemon, garlic, and olive oil, highlighting their natural flavors. Shrimp, mussels, and octopus are popular choices, as well as salted and dried fish like cod and hake.

No Albanian meal is complete without bread, which is served with almost every dish as a staple accompaniment. Traditional Albanian bread, known as bukë, is typically made with wheat flour, water, yeast, and salt, then baked in a wood-fired oven until golden brown and crusty. It is often enjoyed with olive oil, cheese, or jam, and is a comforting and satisfying addition to any meal.

Dairy products also feature prominently in Albanian cuisine, with cheese being a particular favorite among locals. Feta cheese, known as djathë i bardhë, is widely used in salads, pastries, and baked dishes, adding a salty and tangy flavor to the food. Yogurt, or kos, is another staple dairy product, often served as a side dish or used as a base for sauces and marinades.

Albanian cuisine is also known for its wide variety of savory pies and pastries, known as byrek. These flaky, pastry-filled treats can be filled with a variety of ingredients, including cheese, spinach, meat, or potatoes, and are often enjoyed as a snack or appetizer. Another popular pastry is petulla, a fried dough ball served with honey or jam, which is a favorite street food in Albania.

Delving into Albanian Traditional Dishes

Let's take a deep dive into the rich tapestry of Albanian traditional dishes, where centuries-old recipes and culinary techniques come together to create a feast for the senses. Albanian cuisine is a reflection of the country's diverse cultural influences, blending Mediterranean flavors with Balkan and Ottoman traditions to produce dishes that are hearty, flavorful, and satisfying.

One of the most iconic Albanian dishes is tave kosi, a savory baked casserole made with tender lamb or beef, rice, and yogurt. Flavored with garlic, herbs, and sometimes a hint of lemon, tave kosi is a comforting and hearty dish that is often enjoyed during special occasions and family gatherings.

Another beloved Albanian dish is fasule, or bean stew, which is made with white beans, onions, tomatoes, and a variety of spices. Fasule is typically served with crusty bread or rice and is a favorite comfort food among Albanians, especially during the colder months.

For meat lovers, qofte, or meatballs, are a popular choice. Made with minced meat, onions, and spices, qofte are typically grilled or fried and served with a side of fresh vegetables or a salad.

They are a staple of Albanian cuisine and can be found in restaurants, cafes, and street food stalls throughout the country.

Seafood also features prominently in Albanian cuisine, thanks to the country's long coastline along the Adriatic and Ionian Seas. One popular seafood dish is grilled fish, which is typically seasoned with olive oil, lemon, and garlic and served with a side of grilled vegetables or a salad.

No Albanian meal is complete without a side of fresh vegetables, which are often served raw, grilled, or sautéed and flavored with olive oil, lemon, and herbs. Tomatoes, cucumbers, peppers, and eggplants are commonly used in Albanian cooking, as are leafy greens like spinach, kale, and chard.

Albania's rich culinary heritage is also reflected in its wide variety of breads and pastries. Traditional Albanian bread, known as bukë, is typically made with wheat flour, water, yeast, and salt and baked in a wood-fired oven until golden brown and crusty. It is often enjoyed with olive oil, cheese, or jam and is a staple accompaniment to many Albanian dishes.

Iconic Landmarks: Must-See Tourist Sights in Albania

Let's embark on a journey through Albania's iconic landmarks, where ancient history, stunning landscapes, and cultural heritage come together to create unforgettable experiences for travelers. Albania may be a small country, but it is brimming with hidden gems and must-see sights that will captivate and inspire visitors from around the world.

We begin our tour in the capital city of Tirana, where modernity meets tradition in a vibrant and dynamic urban landscape. One of the most iconic landmarks in Tirana is the Skanderbeg Square, named after the national hero Skanderbeg. The square is surrounded by important government buildings, museums, and cultural institutions, including the National History Museum and the National Gallery of Art.

From Tirana, we make our way to the ancient city of Butrint, a UNESCO World Heritage Site located near the southern border of Albania. Butrint is one of the country's most important archaeological sites, boasting ruins dating back to the Greek, Roman, Byzantine, and Venetian periods. Visitors can explore ancient theaters, temples, and fortifications, as well as the impressive Baptistry and Roman Forum.

Next, we journey to the coastal city of Durrës, home to one of the oldest and most important ports in the Adriatic. Durrës is known for its rich history and archaeological treasures, including the Byzantine city walls, the Roman amphitheater, and the Venetian Tower. The city also boasts beautiful beaches and a lively waterfront promenade, making it a popular destination for sun-seekers and history enthusiasts alike.

No visit to Albania would be complete without exploring the stunning landscapes of the Albanian Riviera. This picturesque stretch of coastline along the Ionian Sea is dotted with charming villages, pristine beaches, and hidden coves waiting to be discovered. One of the most iconic landmarks along the Riviera is the Llogara Pass, a winding mountain road that offers breathtaking views of the sea and surrounding mountains.

Further inland, we find the historic town of Gjirokastër, a UNESCO World Heritage Site renowned for its well-preserved Ottoman architecture and traditional stone houses. The highlight of Gjirokastër is the imposing Gjirokastër Castle, which offers panoramic views of the town and surrounding countryside. Visitors can also explore the Ethnographic Museum, housed in a beautifully restored Ottoman-era mansion.

As we conclude our tour of Albania's iconic landmarks, we are reminded of the country's rich cultural heritage and natural beauty, which continue to captivate and inspire visitors from around the world.

UNESCO World Heritage Sites of Albania

Let's delve into the UNESCO World Heritage Sites of Albania, where history, culture, and natural beauty converge to create extraordinary destinations that are recognized for their universal value and significance. Albania may be a small country, but it boasts a rich cultural heritage and a diverse array of landscapes that have earned it a place on the UNESCO World Heritage List.

One of the most iconic UNESCO World Heritage Sites in Albania is the ancient city of Butrint, located near the southern border of the country. Butrint is an archaeological treasure trove, with ruins dating back to the Greek, Roman, Byzantine, and Venetian periods. Visitors can explore ancient theaters, temples, and fortifications, as well as the impressive Baptistry and Roman Forum, offering a fascinating glimpse into Albania's rich history.

Another UNESCO World Heritage Site in Albania is the Historic Centers of Berat and Gjirokastër, two well-preserved Ottoman towns located in the southern part of the country. Berat, also known as the "City of a Thousand Windows," is famous for its white-washed houses, cobbled streets, and picturesque hilltop castle. Gjirokastër, meanwhile, is renowned for its traditional stone houses and imposing Gjirokastër Castle, which offers panoramic views of the surrounding countryside.

The Ancient and Primeval Beech Forests of the Carpathians and Other Regions of Europe, a transnational UNESCO World Heritage Site that includes several countries, also extends into Albania. These pristine beech forests, located in the remote northern part of the country, are home to a rich variety of flora and fauna, including rare and endemic species. Visitors can explore the forests on hiking trails and discover hidden waterfalls, caves, and mountain lakes.

In addition to these cultural and natural sites, Albania is also home to the Butrint National Park, a UNESCO World Heritage Site that encompasses the ancient city of Butrint as well as its surrounding natural landscapes. The park is a haven for wildlife and biodiversity, with diverse ecosystems ranging from wetlands and forests to coastal habitats. Visitors can explore the park on hiking trails, boat tours, and guided archaeological tours, discovering the unique cultural and natural heritage of this remarkable site.

As we explore the UNESCO World Heritage Sites of Albania, we are reminded of the country's rich history, cultural diversity, and natural beauty, which continue to captivate and inspire visitors from around the world.

Tirana: The Vibrant Capital City

Welcome to Tirana, the vibrant capital city of Albania, where history, culture, and modernity collide to create a dynamic urban landscape that captivates visitors from around the world. Situated in the heart of the country, Tirana is not only the political and economic center of Albania but also a bustling metropolis that offers a rich tapestry of experiences for travelers.

At the heart of Tirana lies Skanderbeg Square, named after Albania's national hero, George Kastrioti Skanderbeg. This bustling square serves as the focal point of the city, surrounded by important government buildings, museums, and cultural institutions. The square is a popular gathering place for locals and visitors alike, offering a vibrant atmosphere and plenty of opportunities for people-watching and sightseeing.

One of the most iconic landmarks in Tirana is the Et'hem Bey Mosque, an architectural gem that dates back to the 18th century. Known for its beautiful frescoes and intricate decorations, the mosque is a symbol of Albania's religious diversity and tolerance. Nearby, visitors can explore the Clock Tower of Tirana, which offers panoramic views of the city from its observation deck.

Tirana is also home to a rich cultural scene, with numerous museums, galleries, and theaters that showcase the country's artistic heritage. The National History Museum and the National Gallery of Art are must-visit destinations for history and art enthusiasts, while the Experimental Theater and the National Theater offer performances ranging from classical drama to contemporary dance.

For those seeking a taste of Tirana's culinary delights, the city boasts a diverse array of restaurants, cafes, and eateries that serve up traditional Albanian dishes as well as international cuisine. From cozy neighborhood taverns to chic rooftop bars, Tirana offers dining options to suit every taste and budget.

One of the highlights of Tirana's culinary scene is its vibrant street food culture, with food stalls and vendors serving up a variety of savory and sweet treats on every corner. Don't miss the opportunity to sample local specialties like qofte (meatballs), byrek (savory pastries), and petulla (fried dough balls) as you explore the city streets.

Tirana is also known for its lively nightlife, with a thriving bar and club scene that comes alive after dark. From trendy cocktail bars to underground clubs, Tirana offers plenty of options for those looking to dance the night away or enjoy a leisurely drink with friends.

Shkodër: Gateway to the North

Situated in the northern part of the country, Shkodër is one of Albania's oldest and most important cities, with a rich heritage that dates back thousands of years. One of the highlights of Shkodër is its stunning location on the shores of Lake Shkodër, the largest lake in the Balkans and a haven for wildlife and biodiversity. The lake and its surrounding wetlands are home to a rich variety of bird species, including pelicans, herons, and flamingos, making it a paradise for birdwatchers and nature enthusiasts.

Shkodër is also known for its rich history and cultural heritage, with numerous archaeological sites, museums, and historic landmarks to explore. One of the most iconic landmarks in Shkodër is Rozafa Castle, a medieval fortress that offers panoramic views of the city and surrounding countryside. Legend has it that the castle was built atop the foundations of an ancient Illyrian fortress, and its walls are steeped in centuries of history and legend.

Another must-visit destination in Shkodër is the Marubi National Museum of Photography, which houses one of the largest collections of photographs in the Balkans. The museum showcases the work of the Marubi family, who were pioneers of photography in Albania and documented the country's history and culture from the late 19th century onwards.

Shkodër is also known for its vibrant cultural scene, with numerous festivals, concerts, and events taking place throughout the year. The city is home to several theaters, art galleries, and cultural centers, where visitors can experience traditional Albanian music, dance, and theater performances.

For those looking to explore the natural beauty of the surrounding area, Shkodër serves as a gateway to the Albanian Alps, a rugged mountain range that offers opportunities for hiking, trekking, and outdoor adventure. The nearby Theth and Valbona Valleys are popular destinations for nature lovers, with picturesque villages, crystal-clear rivers, and stunning mountain scenery.

Exploring the Historic Streets of Gjirokastër

Known as the "City of Stone," Gjirokastër is renowned for its well-preserved Ottoman architecture and rich cultural heritage, which have earned it a place on the UNESCO World Heritage List.

As you wander through the narrow streets of Gjirokastër's old town, you'll be transported back in time to a bygone era, where centuries-old buildings and fortifications tell the story of the city's tumultuous history. One of the most iconic landmarks in Gjirokastër is the imposing Gjirokastër Castle, which overlooks the city from its perch atop a hill. Dating back to the 12th century, the castle offers panoramic views of the surrounding countryside and serves as a reminder of Gjirokastër's strategic importance throughout the ages.

Inside the castle walls, visitors can explore a maze of stone corridors, towers, and chambers, discovering hidden courtyards, dungeons, and defensive fortifications along the way. The castle is also home to the Gjirokastër National Museum, which showcases the city's history and cultural heritage through a diverse collection of artifacts, artwork, and historical exhibits.

Outside the castle, the streets of Gjirokastër are lined with traditional stone houses, many of which date back to the Ottoman period. These well-preserved buildings feature distinctive architecture, with wooden balconies, carved doorways, and stone facades that reflect the city's unique blend of Ottoman and Albanian influences. Some of the most notable houses in Gjirokastër, such as the Zekate House and the Skenduli House, have been converted into museums and cultural centers, offering visitors a glimpse into daily life in centuries past.

Gjirokastër is also known for its rich cultural scene, with numerous festivals, concerts, and events taking place throughout the year. The city is home to several theaters, art galleries, and cultural centers, where visitors can experience traditional Albanian music, dance, and theater performances. The Gjirokastër Folklore Festival, held annually in July, is a highlight of the city's cultural calendar, attracting performers and spectators from across Albania and beyond.

Berat: City of a Thousand Windows

Situated along the banks of the Osum River, Berat is one of the oldest continuously inhabited cities in Albania, with a history that dates back over 2,400 years.

One of the most iconic features of Berat is its well-preserved Ottoman houses, which cascade down the slopes of the city's hillsides in a series of terraces, creating a breathtaking panorama of whitewashed facades and red-tiled roofs. These traditional houses, known as kullas, are characterized by their distinctive architecture, with wooden balconies, carved doorways, and rows of windows that give the city its nickname.

The historic center of Berat, known as the Mangalem Quarter, is a UNESCO World Heritage Site and a treasure trove of cultural and architectural landmarks. Here, visitors can explore narrow cobblestone streets, medieval churches, and ancient mosques, discovering hidden courtyards, gardens, and artisan workshops along the way.

One of the most iconic landmarks in Berat is the Berat Castle, a massive fortress that dominates the city skyline from its perch atop a rocky hill. Dating back to the 4th century BC, the castle has undergone numerous renovations and additions over the centuries, with elements from the Byzantine, Ottoman, and Venetian periods still visible today. Inside the castle walls, visitors can explore a maze of narrow alleys, towers, and chambers, as well as the remains of ancient churches, mosques, and a royal palace.

Another must-visit destination in Berat is the Onufri Museum, located inside the 18th-century Church of the Dormition of Saint Mary. The museum houses a rich collection of religious artifacts, icons, and frescoes, including works by the renowned Albanian painter Onufri, after whom the museum is named.

Berat is also known for its rich cultural heritage and vibrant arts scene, with numerous festivals, concerts, and events taking place throughout the year. The city is home to several theaters, art galleries, and cultural centers, where visitors can experience traditional Albanian music, dance, and theater performances.

Durres: Where History Meets the Sea.

Durrës is one of the oldest cities in Albania, with a history that stretches back over 2,600 years. One of the most iconic landmarks in Durrës is the ancient Roman amphitheater, one of the largest and best-preserved amphitheaters in the Balkans. Dating back to the 2nd century AD, the amphitheater once hosted gladiator contests and other spectacles and is now a popular tourist attraction, offering visitors a glimpse into Durrës' rich history.

Another must-visit destination in Durrës is the Durrës Archaeological Museum, which houses a rich collection of artifacts dating back to ancient times. The museum showcases the city's long and storied past, with exhibits ranging from ancient Greek and Roman pottery to Byzantine-era mosaics and sculptures.

Durrës is also known for its beautiful beaches, which stretch for miles along the Adriatic coast, offering plenty of opportunities for sunbathing, swimming, and water sports. The city's waterfront promenade is lined with cafes, bars, and restaurants, making it the perfect place to relax and enjoy the sea breeze.

For those interested in exploring Durrës' maritime history, the Durrës Naval Museum offers a fascinating glimpse into the city's seafaring past. Housed in a historic Venetian tower, the museum features exhibits on shipbuilding, navigation, and maritime trade, as well as artifacts recovered from shipwrecks along the Albanian coast.

Durrës is also home to several other historic landmarks, including the Venetian Tower, the Byzantine Forum, and the Fatih Mosque, which dates back to the 15th century. These architectural treasures reflect the city's diverse cultural heritage and offer visitors a chance to delve deeper into Durrës' past.

As you explore the streets of Durrës, you'll be struck by the city's unique blend of ancient and modern, where historic ruins stand side by side with bustling cafes and shops. Whether you're soaking up the sun on the beach, exploring ancient ruins, or sampling fresh seafood at a seaside restaurant, Durrës offers something for everyone to enjoy.

Vlorë: A Coastal Gem with Rich History

Welcome to Vlorë, a coastal gem nestled along the shores of the Adriatic Sea, where sun-drenched beaches, ancient ruins, and a rich maritime history await visitors from near and far. Situated in the southwestern part of Albania, Vlorë is one of the country's oldest and most important cities, with a history that dates back over 2,500 years.

One of the most iconic landmarks in Vlorë is the Independence Monument, located in the city center overlooking the sea. Erected in 1912, the monument commemorates Albania's declaration of independence from the Ottoman Empire and serves as a symbol of national pride and unity.

Another must-visit destination in Vlorë is the Muradie Mosque, a beautiful Ottoman-era mosque dating back to the 16th century. Situated near the waterfront, the mosque is renowned for its elegant architecture and stunning interior, featuring intricate tilework, ornate calligraphy, and a soaring dome.

Vlorë is also home to several historic landmarks that reflect its rich maritime heritage, including the Kanina Castle, a medieval fortress that overlooks the city from a hilltop perch. Dating back to the 3rd century BC, the castle offers panoramic views of the surrounding countryside and serves as a reminder of Vlorë's strategic importance throughout the ages.

For those interested in exploring Vlorë's natural beauty, the city boasts several beautiful beaches, including the popular Plazhi i Ri and Radhima Beach, which offer pristine sand, crystal-clear waters, and plenty of opportunities for swimming, sunbathing, and water sports.

Vlorë is also known for its vibrant cultural scene, with numerous festivals, concerts, and events taking place throughout the year. The city is home to several theaters, art galleries, and cultural centers, where visitors can experience traditional Albanian music, dance, and theater performances.

As you explore the streets of Vlorë, you'll be struck by the city's unique blend of ancient and modern, where historic landmarks stand side by side with bustling cafes, shops, and restaurants. Whether you're soaking up the sun on the beach, exploring ancient ruins, or sampling fresh seafood at a seaside restaurant, Vlorë offers something for everyone to enjoy.

Korçë: Cultural Capital of Albania

Situated amidst rolling hills and lush landscapes, Korçë has long been considered a center of learning, creativity, and intellectual pursuits. One of the most iconic landmarks in Korçë is the Resurrection Cathedral, an impressive Orthodox cathedral that dominates the city skyline with its imposing dome and elegant architecture. Built in the early 20th century, the cathedral is renowned for its beautiful frescoes, intricate iconography, and stunning interior, making it a must-visit destination for visitors to Korçë.

Korçë is also home to several other historic churches and religious sites, including the Old Bazaar Mosque, the Iljaz Mirahori Mosque, and the Church of Saint George, which date back to the Ottoman and Byzantine periods and reflect the city's diverse cultural and religious heritage.

For those interested in exploring Korçë's cultural heritage, the National Museum of Medieval Art offers a fascinating glimpse into the city's past, with a rich collection of religious icons, manuscripts, and artifacts dating back to the Middle Ages. The museum showcases the artistic and cultural achievements of the region, including works by renowned Albanian artists such as Onufri and David Selenica.

Korçë is also known for its vibrant arts scene, with numerous galleries, theaters, and cultural institutions that showcase the work of local and international artists. The Korçë National Theater is a hub of creative activity, with regular performances of theater, music, and dance that attract audiences from across Albania and beyond.

In addition to its cultural attractions, Korçë is also a culinary destination, known for its delicious cuisine and traditional Albanian dishes. The city's bustling markets and local eateries offer a wide variety of fresh produce, meats, cheeses, and baked goods, allowing visitors to sample the flavors of the region and experience the warmth and hospitality of its people.

Krujë: Home of Albania's National Hero

Welcome to Krujë, a historic city nestled in the mountains of central Albania, renowned as the home of Albania's national hero, Skanderbeg. Situated just 20 miles north of the capital, Tirana, Krujë is steeped in history and tradition, with a rich cultural heritage that dates back over a thousand years.

The most iconic landmark in Krujë is the Krujë Castle, a medieval fortress perched atop a rocky hill overlooking the city and the surrounding countryside. Built in the 5th century AD, the castle played a central role in Albania's resistance against the Ottoman Empire, serving as the stronghold of Skanderbeg during his legendary defense against Ottoman invasion in the 15th century.

Inside the castle walls, visitors can explore a maze of courtyards, towers, and ramparts, as well as the Skanderbeg Museum, which is dedicated to the life and legacy of Albania's national hero. The museum showcases artifacts, weapons, and armor from Skanderbeg's era, as well as exhibits on Albanian history, culture, and folklore.

Another must-visit destination in Krujë is the Krujë Old Bazaar, a bustling marketplace that has been a center of trade and commerce for centuries. Here, visitors can browse a wide variety of stalls selling traditional handicrafts, souvenirs, and locally-made goods, as well as sample delicious Albanian cuisine at one of the many cafes and restaurants lining the cobblestone streets.

Krujë is also home to several historic mosques and religious sites, including the Fatih Sultan Mehmet Mosque, which dates back to the 18th century and is one of the oldest mosques in Albania. The mosque is renowned for its beautiful architecture and intricate tilework, reflecting the city's rich cultural and religious diversity.

In addition to its cultural attractions, Krujë is also known for its stunning natural beauty, with picturesque mountain landscapes, lush forests, and crystal-clear streams that offer plenty of opportunities for outdoor adventure and exploration.

Albanian Festivals and Traditions

One of the most important festivals in Albania is the Albanian Independence Day, celebrated on November 28th to commemorate the country's declaration of independence from the Ottoman Empire in 1912. This national holiday is marked by parades, concerts, and fireworks displays, as well as speeches and ceremonies honoring Albania's history and heritage.

Another major festival in Albania is the Feast of Saint George, celebrated on April 23rd in honor of the country's patron saint. This religious holiday is observed with church services, processions, and traditional feasts, as well as cultural events and performances that showcase Albania's Christian heritage.

One of the most colorful and vibrant festivals in Albania is the Albanian Folklore Festival, held annually in Gjirokastër in July. This lively event brings together folk dance groups, musicians, and performers from across Albania and the Balkans, who come to showcase their traditional music, dance, and costumes in a celebration of cultural diversity and unity.

In addition to religious and cultural festivals, Albania is also known for its unique traditions and customs that have been passed down through generations. One such tradition is the Albanian wedding ceremony, which is a joyous and festive occasion that typically lasts for several days and involves music, dancing, feasting, and elaborate rituals.

Another important tradition in Albania is the celebration of the Albanian New Year, known as Dita e Verës or "Summer Day," which is celebrated on March 14th according to the traditional Albanian calendar. This ancient pagan holiday marks the arrival of spring and is celebrated with outdoor picnics, bonfires, and festive gatherings.

Throughout the year, Albanians also celebrate a variety of local festivals and holidays that are unique to their region or community, ranging from harvest festivals and religious pilgrimages to village fairs and cultural exhibitions.

As you explore the rich tapestry of Albanian festivals and traditions, you'll be struck by the warmth, hospitality, and sense of community that pervades every celebration, making it a truly unforgettable experience.

Folk Music and Dance: Cultural Expressions of Albania

In Albania, folk music and dance hold a special place in the hearts of the people, serving as a powerful means of preserving heritage, celebrating community, and expressing identity. Albanian folk music is incredibly diverse, with distinct regional styles and influences that reflect the country's rich cultural heritage and geographic diversity. Traditional Albanian music features a wide variety of instruments, including the çifteli (a stringed instrument), lahuta (a bowed instrument), and gajda (a type of bagpipe), as well as percussion instruments like the daulle (a type of drum) and def (a frame drum).

One of the most iconic forms of Albanian folk music is the iso-polyphony, a unique style of vocal harmony that is recognized by UNESCO as a Masterpiece of the Oral and Intangible Heritage of Humanity. Iso-polyphony is characterized by the use of multiple vocal parts, sung in parallel intervals, creating a rich and intricate tapestry of sound that is both haunting and beautiful.

In addition to vocal music, Albanian folk dance is also an integral part of the country's cultural heritage, with a wide variety of traditional dances that are performed at weddings, festivals, and other celebrations. Each region of Albania has its own unique dance traditions, with distinctive costumes, choreography, and rhythms that reflect the local culture and history.

One of the most famous Albanian folk dances is the Valle, a lively circle dance that is performed by both men and women and is often accompanied by traditional music played on instruments like the clarinet, accordion, and violin. The Valle is a joyous and energetic dance, with intricate footwork and movements that vary from region to region.

Another popular Albanian folk dance is the Vallja e Rugovës, a ceremonial dance that originated in the Rugova Valley of Kosovo and is characterized by its slow, graceful movements and intricate patterns. The Vallja e Rugovës is often performed at weddings and other special occasions, and is accompanied by traditional music played on instruments like the zurna (a type of flute) and dajre (a tambourine). As you immerse yourself in the world of Albanian folk music and dance, you'll be captivated by the beauty, passion, and diversity of this vibrant cultural tradition.

Albanian Art and Craftsmanship Through the Ages

Throughout the ages, Albania has been home to a diverse array of artistic styles and techniques, reflecting the country's unique cultural heritage and geographic diversity. One of the earliest forms of Albanian art is Illyrian art, which dates back to ancient times and is characterized by its distinctive motifs and symbols, including geometric patterns, animal designs, and stylized human figures. Illyrian art encompassed a wide range of mediums, including pottery, metalwork, and sculpture, and played a central role in shaping the artistic identity of the region.

With the arrival of Christianity in Albania, Byzantine art and iconography became prominent, influencing both religious and secular art forms. Byzantine art is characterized by its rich colors, intricate patterns, and spiritual themes, with icons and frescoes adorning churches, monasteries, and other religious buildings throughout Albania.

During the Ottoman period, Albanian art experienced a period of flourishing creativity and innovation, with influences from both the Islamic and European worlds. Ottoman-era Albanian art is characterized by its ornate decoration, intricate calligraphy, and geometric designs, which can be seen in everything from architecture and textiles to ceramics and metalwork.

In the 19th and early 20th centuries, Albania underwent a period of cultural revival known as the National Awakening, which saw a renewed interest in Albanian identity, language, and culture. This cultural renaissance gave rise to a new wave of Albanian art and craftsmanship, with artists and artisans drawing inspiration from traditional folk motifs and themes to create works that celebrated the spirit of the Albanian people.

In the modern era, Albanian art continues to evolve and thrive, with contemporary artists and craftsmen drawing inspiration from both the country's rich cultural heritage and the global art scene. Today, Albania is home to a vibrant community of artists, sculptors, painters, and craftsmen who are pushing the boundaries of creativity and innovation in their respective fields. As you explore the world of Albanian art and craftsmanship, you'll be captivated by the beauty, diversity, and richness of this vibrant cultural tradition.

The Impact of Religion on Albanian Culture

Albania's religious landscape is characterized by a unique blend of religious diversity and tolerance, shaped by centuries of historical, political, and cultural influences. One of the defining features of Albanian religious history is its long tradition of religious pluralism, where different religious communities have coexisted peacefully for centuries. The country is home to three major religious groups: Islam, Christianity (both Catholic and Orthodox), and a small minority of other faiths, including Bektashi and Judaism.

Islam has deep roots in Albania, with the majority of Albanians adhering to Sunni Islam, which was introduced to the region during the Ottoman period. However, Albanian Islam is unique in its interpretation and practice, with a strong tradition of religious tolerance and syncretism that has shaped the country's cultural identity.

Christianity also has a strong presence in Albania, with significant Catholic and Orthodox communities spread throughout the country. The Albanian Orthodox Church, part of the Eastern Orthodox tradition, has a rich history dating back to ancient times and continues to play an important role in the cultural and religious life of the country.

The Catholic Church also has a long history in Albania, with roots dating back to the medieval period and a significant presence in the northern part of the country. Catholicism has had a profound influence on Albanian culture, particularly in areas such as education, healthcare, and social welfare.

In addition to Islam and Christianity, Albania is also home to the Bektashi Order, a Sufi Muslim sect that has a significant presence in the country. The Bektashi Order is known for its emphasis on spirituality, tolerance, and social justice, and has played a key role in shaping Albanian religious and cultural identity.

Despite its religious diversity, Albania is known for its tradition of religious tolerance and coexistence, where people of different faiths live and work together in harmony. This spirit of tolerance is deeply rooted in Albanian culture and is reflected in the country's laws, institutions, and social norms. As you explore the impact of religion on Albanian culture, you'll be struck by the resilience, adaptability, and diversity of faith traditions that have shaped the country's identity over the centuries.

Albanian Hospitality: A Warm Welcome Awaits

Hospitality is deeply ingrained in Albanian culture, with traditions of welcoming guests and treating them like family dating back centuries. In Albania, hospitality is more than just a gesture—it's a way of life. From the moment you arrive, you'll be greeted with open arms and genuine warmth, as Albanians take pride in making visitors feel at home. Whether you're staying in a small village or a bustling city, you'll find that hospitality is a universal language that transcends barriers of language and culture.

One of the hallmarks of Albanian hospitality is the tradition of "xhiro," or taking a leisurely stroll through the neighborhood in the evening. This social custom is a way for neighbors to connect, catch up on news, and extend hospitality to one another, often inviting passersby to join them for a cup of coffee or a glass of raki.

Albanian hospitality is also expressed through food, with guests being treated to an abundance of delicious homemade dishes and traditional specialties. Meals in Albania are a communal affair, with friends and family gathering around the table to share stories, laughter, and of course, plenty of food. Albanian cuisine is known for its hearty, flavorful dishes, including grilled meats, fresh seafood, and an array of savory pastries and desserts.

In addition to food, Albanian hospitality also extends to accommodations, with visitors often being welcomed into the homes of locals for a truly authentic experience. Whether you're staying in a guesthouse, a hostel, or a private home, you'll find that Albanian hosts go out of their way to ensure that you feel comfortable and cared for during your stay.

But perhaps the most memorable aspect of Albanian hospitality is the genuine warmth and friendliness of the people themselves. Albanians are known for their hospitality, generosity, and kindness, and you'll find that strangers quickly become friends in this welcoming country. Whether you're exploring ancient ruins, hiking through the mountains, or simply strolling through the streets, you'll be met with smiles, greetings, and invitations to join in the local festivities.

As you experience the warmth and hospitality of Albania, you'll come to understand why it's known as the Land of Eagles and the Land of Hospitality—a place where every guest is treated like family and every visit is an opportunity to forge lasting memories and friendships.

Understanding Albanian Social Etiquette

In Albania, social etiquette plays a significant role in daily interactions, reflecting the values of respect, hospitality, and community that are deeply ingrained in Albanian culture. Understanding Albanian social etiquette can help visitors navigate social situations with ease and show appreciation for the country's customs and traditions.

One of the most important aspects of Albanian social etiquette is the emphasis on hospitality and generosity. When visiting someone's home, it is customary to bring a small gift, such as flowers, chocolates, or pastries, as a token of appreciation for the host's hospitality. Guests are typically greeted warmly and offered refreshments, and it is considered polite to accept these offerings with gratitude.

In social settings, Albanians place a high value on politeness and respect, particularly towards elders and authority figures. It is customary to address people using formal titles, such as "Zoti" (Mr.) or "Zonja" (Mrs.), followed by their last name, until invited to use their first name. Additionally, it is common to greet people with a handshake and maintain eye contact during conversations as a sign of respect. Albanians also place great importance on family and community, and social gatherings often revolve around these relationships. Family ties are strong in Albanian culture, and it is not uncommon for extended family members to live together or remain closely connected throughout their lives. Respect for elders is paramount, and younger family members are expected to show deference and obedience to their elders. In terms of dining etiquette, it is customary to wait for the host to begin eating before starting your meal. It is also polite to compliment the host on the food and express gratitude for their hospitality. When dining in a restaurant, it is customary to leave a small tip as a token of appreciation for the service.

When visiting religious sites or participating in religious ceremonies, it is important to dress modestly and show respect for the customs and traditions of the faith community. In mosques, women are typically expected to cover their heads with a scarf, and both men and women should remove their shoes before entering.

Overall, Albanian social etiquette is rooted in the values of respect, hospitality, and community, and visitors who take the time to understand and appreciate these customs will find themselves warmly welcomed into the fold of Albanian society. By embracing the social etiquette of Albania, travelers can forge meaningful connections, gain deeper insights into the culture, and create lasting memories of their time in this beautiful Balkan nation.

Family Life and Values in Albania

In Albanian culture, family plays a central role in shaping individual identity and social dynamics, and the strength of family ties is evident in all aspects of life. Family is the cornerstone of Albanian society, with strong bonds between parents, children, grandparents, and extended relatives forming the foundation of social structure. Albanian families are typically close-knit and multigenerational, with multiple generations often living together or in close proximity to one another. This fosters a sense of unity, support, and shared responsibility within the family unit.

One of the defining features of Albanian family life is the concept of "fis," or clan, which refers to a group of related families who share a common ancestry and heritage. The fis provides a sense of belonging and identity for its members, who come together to celebrate holidays, commemorate important events, and support one another in times of need.

In Albanian culture, the role of the family extends beyond the nuclear family unit to include the broader community of relatives and kin. This extended family network provides a support system for individuals throughout their lives, offering emotional, financial, and practical assistance when needed.

Gender roles within Albanian families are often traditional, with men typically serving as the primary breadwinners and women assuming responsibility for household chores and childcare. However, these roles are evolving, particularly in urban areas and among younger generations, as more women enter the workforce and contribute to the family's financial stability.

Education is highly valued in Albanian families, with parents placing a strong emphasis on academic achievement and personal development. Children are encouraged to pursue higher education and career opportunities, with parents often making significant sacrifices to ensure their children have access to educational resources and opportunities.

Religion also plays a significant role in Albanian family life, with many families participating in religious rituals, ceremonies, and observances together. Religious values such as compassion, forgiveness, and humility are instilled in children from a young age, shaping their moral and ethical development.

Overall, family life in Albania is characterized by love, support, and solidarity, with families serving as the bedrock of society and the source of strength and resilience for individuals. By exploring the dynamics of family life and values in Albania, we gain a deeper understanding of the cultural richness and social fabric of this vibrant Balkan nation.

Education System in Albania: Past and Present

The education system in Albania has undergone significant transformations over the years, reflecting changes in political ideology, social priorities, and economic development. Historically, education in Albania was limited and largely inaccessible to the general population. During the Ottoman period, education was primarily provided by religious institutions, such as madrasas and monasteries, and was reserved for the elite classes and clergy. However, with the rise of nationalism and the struggle for independence in the late 19th and early 20th centuries, efforts were made to expand access to education and promote literacy among the general population.

Following Albania's declaration of independence in 1912, the government launched initiatives to establish a modern education system that would promote national identity, language, and culture. The first Albanian-language schools were opened, and efforts were made to standardize the Albanian language and curriculum. However, progress was slow, and education remained largely underfunded and underdeveloped for much of the early 20th century.

The education system underwent significant changes during the communist era under the leadership of Enver Hoxha, who prioritized education as a means of promoting socialist ideology and building a modern, industrialized society. During this time, education was made compulsory and free for all children, and significant investments were made in school infrastructure, teacher training, and curriculum development. However, education was also heavily politicized, with an emphasis on ideological indoctrination and conformity to state ideology.

Following the collapse of communism in the early 1990s, Albania transitioned to a democratic system of government and embarked on a period of political and economic reform. The education system underwent significant changes during this time, with efforts to modernize curriculum, improve teacher training, and expand access to education at all levels. Today, education in Albania is governed by the Ministry of Education, Sports, and Youth, which oversees a system of public and private schools, as well as vocational and higher education institutions.

Despite progress, challenges remain in the Albanian education system, including issues of quality, equity, and access. Rural areas and marginalized communities continue to face barriers to education, and disparities in educational outcomes persist between urban and rural areas, as well as between different socioeconomic groups. Additionally, the education system continues to grapple with issues of corruption, nepotism, and political interference, which can undermine the quality and integrity of education.

As Albania continues to navigate the challenges and opportunities of the 21st century, the education system will play a critical role in shaping the future of the country and its people. By investing in education, fostering innovation, and promoting inclusive and equitable access to learning opportunities, Albania can empower its citizens to reach their full potential and contribute to the social, economic, and cultural development of the nation.

Exploring the Rich Literary Heritage of Albania

Albania boasts a long and illustrious literary history, with roots that date back to ancient times and a diverse array of literary genres, styles, and voices that reflect the country's unique cultural heritage and linguistic richness. One of the earliest forms of Albanian literature is oral poetry, which has been passed down through generations via folk songs, epic poems, and ballads. These ancient oral traditions played a central role in preserving Albania's cultural identity and history, with epic poems like the "Këngë Kreshnikësh" (Songs of the Frontier Warriors) and "Lahuta e Malcís" (The Highland Lute) celebrating the heroic deeds and struggles of the Albanian people.

The written literary tradition in Albania began to emerge in the 15th century with the advent of the Albanian alphabet, which was developed by Gjon Buzuku in his "Meshari" (Missal), one of the earliest known books written in Albanian. Over the centuries, Albanian literature flourished, with writers and poets producing works in a variety of genres, including poetry, prose, drama, and essays.

One of the most celebrated figures in Albanian literature is the national poet Naim Frashëri, whose poetry is regarded as a cornerstone of Albanian literary tradition. Frashëri's works, including his epic poem "Lulet e Verës" (The Flowers of

Spring), are noted for their lyrical beauty, philosophical depth, and patriotic themes, and have had a profound influence on generations of Albanian writers and intellectuals.

In the 20th century, Albanian literature experienced a period of intense creativity and innovation, with writers and poets exploring themes of identity, politics, and social change. Figures like Ismail Kadare, Albania's most internationally acclaimed writer, gained recognition for their powerful and thought-provoking novels, which often delve into the complexities of Albanian history and society.

Despite periods of political censorship and repression, Albanian literature has continued to thrive, with writers and poets finding creative ways to navigate the challenges of authoritarian rule and censorship. Today, Albania boasts a vibrant literary scene, with a diverse array of voices and perspectives contributing to the country's rich literary tapestry.

As you explore the rich literary heritage of Albania, you'll be captivated by the beauty, depth, and complexity of its literary traditions, and gain a deeper appreciation for the role that literature plays in shaping the cultural identity and collective consciousness of the Albanian people.

The Resilience of Albanian Language and Alphabet

The Albanian language is one of the oldest and most distinctive languages in Europe, with roots that can be traced back to ancient times. It belongs to the Indo-European language family, but its precise origins and relationship to other languages remain a subject of debate among linguists.

One of the most remarkable aspects of the Albanian language is its unique alphabet, known as the Albanian alphabet or "alfabeti shqip." The Albanian alphabet is descended from the ancient Illyrian script, which was used by the Illyrian people, an ancient Indo-European tribe that inhabited the Balkans thousands of years ago. The modern Albanian alphabet was officially standardized in the early 20th century, with the publication of the "Fjalori i Gjuhës Shqipe" (Dictionary of the Albanian Language) by linguist Faik Konica.

The Albanian alphabet consists of 36 letters, including 28 letters of the Latin alphabet and an additional eight letters with diacritical marks, which represent sounds unique to the Albanian language. The alphabet is phonetic, meaning that each letter corresponds to a specific sound, making it relatively easy to learn and pronounce for speakers of other languages.

Despite centuries of foreign rule and cultural influence, the Albanian language and alphabet have remained remarkably resilient, serving as symbols of national identity and pride for the Albanian people. Throughout history, efforts have been made to preserve and promote the Albanian language, including the establishment of Albanian-language schools, the publication of literary works in Albanian, and the development of language standards and norms.

During periods of foreign occupation and oppression, the Albanian language and alphabet faced challenges and threats to their survival, including attempts to suppress or assimilate the language into dominant cultural and linguistic norms. However, the Albanian people have steadfastly defended their language and alphabet, resisting efforts to erode their linguistic and cultural heritage.

Today, the Albanian language and alphabet are thriving, with millions of speakers around the world and a rich literary and cultural tradition that continues to inspire and captivate audiences both at home and abroad. The resilience of the Albanian language and alphabet is a testament to the strength and perseverance of the Albanian people, who have overcome adversity and adversity to preserve their unique linguistic and cultural identity.

Glimpses into Albanian Folklore and Mythology

Albanian folklore is a rich tapestry of myths, legends, and superstitions that reflect the country's rich history, diverse cultural influences, and deep connection to the natural world. At the heart of Albanian folklore are a myriad of mythical creatures, heroes, and spirits that inhabit the mountains, forests, and rivers of the land. One of the most iconic figures in Albanian folklore is the "bukuroshe," or fairy, a beautiful and benevolent spirit who is said to dwell in the mountains and forests, protecting travelers and granting wishes to those who are pure of heart.

Another prominent figure in Albanian folklore is the "djall," or devil, a malevolent spirit who is believed to lurk in the shadows, tempting humans with promises of wealth and power in exchange for their souls. According to legend, the djall takes on various forms and disguises, appearing to unsuspecting victims in moments of weakness or desperation.

Albanian folklore is also rich in tales of legendary heroes and warriors who embody the virtues of courage, honor, and resilience. One of the most famous heroes in Albanian folklore is Gjergj Elez Alia, a mythical warrior who is celebrated for his bravery and prowess in battle. Legend has it that Gjergj Elez Alia possessed superhuman strength and agility, and that he single-handedly defended Albania against foreign invaders.

In addition to mythical creatures and legendary heroes, Albanian folklore is replete with stories of supernatural phenomena and magical rituals that have been passed down through generations. From tales of witches and sorcerers to practices of divination and herbal medicine, Albanian folklore offers a glimpse into a world where the boundaries between the natural and the supernatural are blurred.

One of the most enduring aspects of Albanian folklore is its connection to nature and the elements. Many Albanian myths and legends are centered around natural landmarks such as mountains, rivers, and caves, which are believed to be inhabited by spirits and deities. The natural world is revered and respected in Albanian folklore, with rituals and ceremonies often performed to honor the spirits of the land and ensure a bountiful harvest.

As you delve into the rich tapestry of Albanian folklore and mythology, you'll be transported to a world of wonder and imagination, where ancient beliefs and traditions continue to shape the cultural identity of the Albanian people.

Albanian Diaspora: Keeping Traditions Alive Abroad

The Albanian diaspora refers to the communities of Albanian expatriates and descendants living abroad, who have migrated from Albania, Kosovo, Macedonia, and other regions with significant Albanian populations, to countries around the world.

The Albanian diaspora has its roots in centuries of migration and movement, driven by economic, political, and social factors. Historically, Albanians have migrated to neighboring countries in search of better economic opportunities, escaping political persecution, or seeking refuge from conflict and instability. In more recent times, Albanians have also migrated to Western Europe, North America, Australia, and other regions in search of work, education, and a better quality of life.

One of the defining features of the Albanian diaspora is its strong sense of identity and cultural pride. Despite being scattered across different continents and countries, Albanian expatriates and descendants have maintained a strong connection to their cultural heritage and homeland, preserving traditions, language, and customs passed down through generations.

In diaspora communities around the world, Albanians have established cultural organizations, community centers, and religious institutions to celebrate their heritage and foster a sense of belonging and solidarity. These organizations play a vital role in preserving Albanian traditions and values, organizing cultural events, festivals, and gatherings, and providing support and resources to newcomers and immigrants.

Language is an important aspect of Albanian identity, and efforts have been made to ensure that the Albanian language is preserved and promoted within diaspora communities. Albanian-language schools, classes, and programs have been established in many countries to teach the language to children and adults, ensuring that future generations maintain fluency in their mother tongue.

Religion also plays a significant role in the Albanian diaspora, with Orthodox, Catholic, and Muslim communities maintaining religious practices, rituals, and traditions passed down from their ancestors. Religious institutions and organizations provide spiritual guidance, support, and community services to Albanians living abroad, helping to strengthen their sense of identity and connection to their cultural heritage.

Despite the challenges of assimilation, discrimination, and cultural adaptation, the Albanian diaspora has remained resilient and resourceful, maintaining strong ties to their homeland while embracing the opportunities and challenges of life abroad. Through their contributions to society, economy, and culture, Albanian expatriates and descendants continue to enrich the global community and keep the traditions of their homeland alive for future generations.

The Albanian Revival: National Awakening in the 19th Century

The 19th century saw Albania emerge from centuries of foreign rule and occupation, with the Ottoman Empire exerting control over much of the Balkan region, including Albanian territories.

During this time, Albania experienced a cultural and intellectual awakening, fueled by a growing sense of national identity and pride among the Albanian people. Influenced by the ideals of European nationalism and enlightenment, Albanian intellectuals, writers, and activists began to advocate for the preservation and promotion of Albanian language, culture, and traditions.

One of the key figures of the Albanian Revival was the Albanian national hero, Gjergj Kastrioti Skanderbeg, who led a successful rebellion against the Ottoman Empire in the 15th century. Skanderbeg's legacy served as a source of inspiration and symbol of resistance for generations of Albanians, who looked to him as a symbol of Albanian unity and independence.

The 19th century also saw the emergence of Albanian-language literature and journalism, with writers and poets such as Naim Frashëri,

Sami Frashëri, and Pashko Vasa playing a prominent role in promoting Albanian language and culture. The publication of the first Albanian-language newspaper, "Shqipëria e Re" (New Albania), in 1889 marked a significant milestone in the Albanian Revival, providing a platform for the dissemination of nationalist ideas and cultural expression.

Albanian intellectuals and activists also began to organize and mobilize for political autonomy and independence, forming secret societies and underground movements to resist Ottoman rule and advocate for Albanian interests. One such organization was the League of Prizren, founded in 1878, which sought to unite Albanian-inhabited territories under a single autonomous state.

The Albanian Revival was not without its challenges and setbacks, as the Ottoman Empire and other foreign powers sought to suppress Albanian nationalism and maintain control over Albanian territories. The Congress of Berlin in 1878, which redrawn the borders of the Balkans, further complicated efforts for Albanian independence, as Albanian-inhabited territories were divided among neighboring states.

Despite these obstacles, the Albanian Revival laid the foundation for the modern Albanian state and the eventual declaration of Albanian independence in 1912. The spirit of nationalism and cultural revival that emerged in the 19th century continues to inspire and inform the identity and aspirations of the Albanian people today, serving as a testament to the enduring resilience and determination of a nation striving for freedom and self-determination.

World War II and Albania's Role in the Resistance

The war brought unprecedented turmoil and upheaval to Albania, as the country found itself caught in the crossfire of competing geopolitical interests and faced with the challenge of maintaining its sovereignty and independence.

Albania was initially invaded and occupied by Italy in April 1939, as part of Mussolini's expansionist ambitions in the Balkans. The Italian occupation brought hardship and repression to the Albanian people, who endured economic exploitation, political oppression, and cultural assimilation under Italian rule.

In September 1943, following the collapse of Mussolini's regime and Italy's surrender to the Allied powers, Germany seized control of Albania and established a puppet government under the leadership of the nationalist politician, Xhafer Deva. The German occupation intensified the suffering of the Albanian people, as they faced widespread violence, persecution, and forced labor at the hands of Nazi forces.

Despite the overwhelming odds, Albania's resistance movement, known as the National Liberation Movement (NLMA), emerged as a formidable force against Axis occupiers. Led by the Communist Party of Albania, under the leadership of Enver Hoxha, the NLMA mobilized Albanian citizens from all walks of life to join the fight against fascism and foreign domination.

The Albanian resistance was characterized by its guerrilla warfare tactics, sabotage operations, and acts of sabotage against Axis forces and collaborators. Partisan fighters, known as "partizanët," waged a relentless campaign of resistance in the mountains, forests, and villages of Albania, launching ambushes, raids, and attacks against enemy targets.

One of the most significant battles of the Albanian resistance was the Battle of Çermenika in October 1944, where Albanian partisans, with the support of Allied forces, successfully repelled a German offensive and inflicted heavy casualties on Axis troops. The victory at Çermenika marked a turning point in the Albanian resistance and paved the way for the liberation of Albania from Axis occupation.

In November 1944, the Albanian partisans, supported by Allied forces, launched a final offensive against German forces, liberating Tirana and other major cities from Axis control. The liberation of Albania brought an end to four years of brutal occupation and marked the beginning of a new chapter in the country's history.

The legacy of Albania's resistance movement continues to be celebrated as a symbol of national unity, sacrifice, and resilience. The courage and determination of Albanian partisans in the face of overwhelming odds serve as a testament to the indomitable spirit of the Albanian people and their unwavering commitment to freedom and independence.

Albania in the Cold War Era: Isolation and Transition

Following World War II, Albania emerged as a communist state under the leadership of Enver Hoxha and the Communist Party of Albania (later renamed the Party of Labour of Albania). Albania's relationship with the Soviet Union and other Eastern Bloc countries quickly soured, as Hoxha pursued a policy of "self-reliance" and "socialism in one country," rejecting the influence of both the Soviet and Chinese Communist regimes. In 1961, Albania officially withdrew from the Warsaw Pact, further isolating itself from the Soviet sphere of influence and aligning more closely with China.

The Hoxha regime implemented a series of radical reforms aimed at transforming Albanian society along strict Marxist-Leninist lines. These reforms included collectivization of agriculture, nationalization of industry, and the establishment of a centralized command economy. The government also carried out purges and repression against perceived enemies of the state, including political dissidents, intellectuals, and religious leaders.

Albania's isolationist policies and repressive measures led to a closed society characterized by strict censorship, limited contact with the outside world, and a pervasive culture of fear and suspicion. The government tightly controlled all aspects of public life, including the media, education, and cultural institutions, to maintain its grip on power.

Despite its isolation, Albania did receive support from China, which provided economic aid, military assistance, and ideological guidance to the Hoxha regime. However, Albania's dependence on China strained relations between the two countries, leading to tensions and disagreements over ideological and strategic matters.

The collapse of communism in Eastern Europe in the late 1980s and early 1990s had a profound impact on Albania, as popular discontent and demands for political reform began to grow. In 1991, following mass protests and demonstrations, the Hoxha regime was overthrown, and Albania embarked on a transition to democracy and market economy.

The end of the Cold War and the collapse of communism in Albania marked the beginning of a new era of political, social, and economic change. The country faced numerous challenges during its transition, including political instability, economic hardship, and social upheaval. However, Albania also embraced newfound freedoms and opportunities, as it sought to integrate into the global community and chart a new course for its future.

Albania's Journey to European Integration

Since the collapse of communism in the early 1990s, Albania has embarked on a path of reform and transformation aimed at aligning itself with European standards and values and ultimately joining the European Union.

The journey toward European integration began in earnest in 2000, when Albania signed the Stabilization and Association Agreement (SAA) with the European Union, laying the groundwork for closer political, economic, and institutional cooperation. The SAA provided a framework for Albania to undertake comprehensive reforms in areas such as democracy, rule of law, human rights, and market economy.

Over the years, Albania has made significant progress in implementing reforms and meeting the criteria set forth by the European Union for membership. The country has undertaken extensive legislative and institutional reforms aimed at strengthening democratic institutions, promoting good governance, and combating corruption and organized crime.

Albania has also made strides in improving its economic governance and creating a more favorable business environment for investment and growth. Efforts to modernize infrastructure, enhance public administration, and promote economic diversification have been key priorities in Albania's quest for European integration.

One of the major milestones in Albania's journey to European integration was the granting of candidate status by the European Council in 2014, which recognized Albania's progress in meeting the requirements for EU membership. This milestone provided a renewed impetus for Albania to accelerate reforms and deepen its engagement with the European Union.

Despite progress, Albania still faces significant challenges on the path to European integration. Key areas requiring further attention include strengthening the rule of law, addressing judicial reform, improving public administration, and combating corruption and organized crime. The European Union has called for sustained efforts and tangible results in these areas as prerequisites for further progress toward membership.

Albania's journey to European integration is also influenced by regional dynamics and geopolitical considerations. The country's strategic location in the Western Balkans makes it a key player in regional cooperation and stability efforts. Albania's commitment to regional cooperation and reconciliation is essential for fostering peace, security, and prosperity in the Balkans and advancing the European integration agenda.

As Albania continues its journey toward European integration, it faces both opportunities and challenges on the road ahead. The country's determination, resilience, and commitment to European values will be crucial in overcoming obstacles and realizing its aspirations for a future within the European Union.

Environmental Challenges and Conservation Efforts

Albania's diverse landscapes, ranging from rugged mountains to pristine coastlines, support a wealth of ecosystems, wildlife, and plant species, making it a biodiversity hotspot in the Balkans. However, rapid urbanization, industrialization, deforestation, pollution, and unsustainable land use practices pose serious threats to Albania's environment and natural resources. One of the most pressing environmental challenges facing Albania is deforestation, driven by illegal logging, agricultural expansion, and urban development. Deforestation not only destroys vital habitats for wildlife but also contributes to soil erosion, landslides, and loss of biodiversity.

Pollution is another major environmental concern in Albania, particularly in urban areas and industrial zones. Poor waste management practices, inadequate wastewater treatment, and air pollution from vehicles and industries contribute to environmental degradation and pose risks to human health. Efforts to address pollution and improve environmental quality are hindered by limited resources, weak enforcement of environmental regulations, and lack of public awareness and participation.

Albania's rich biodiversity is also under threat from habitat destruction, poaching, and illegal wildlife trade. Protected areas, such as national parks and nature reserves, play a crucial role in conserving Albania's natural heritage and providing habitat for endangered species. However, these areas face challenges such as insufficient funding, inadequate management, and encroachment by human activities.

Despite these challenges, Albania has made progress in recent years in implementing environmental policies and initiatives to address conservation priorities and promote sustainable development. The government has adopted laws and regulations to protect natural habitats, regulate land use, and promote renewable energy sources. Albania is also actively engaged in international conservation efforts and has ratified various environmental treaties and agreements to protect biodiversity and mitigate climate change.

Community-based conservation projects and grassroots initiatives are also emerging as important tools for environmental protection and sustainable development in Albania. Local communities, NGOs, and civil society organizations are working together to raise awareness, promote environmental education, and implement conservation projects at the grassroots level.

Albania's journey toward environmental sustainability and conservation is ongoing, requiring continued commitment, collaboration, and innovation from all stakeholders. By addressing environmental challenges, protecting natural resources, and promoting sustainable development, Albania can safeguard its natural heritage for future generations and contribute to global efforts to address environmental issues and climate change.

Albanian Economy: Opportunities and Challenges

Since the transition from communism in the early 1990s, Albania has undergone significant economic reforms aimed at transitioning from a centrally planned to a market-oriented economy.

Albania's economy has experienced steady growth over the past two decades, driven by reforms aimed at attracting foreign investment, promoting private sector development, and integrating into the global economy. The country's strategic location in the Western Balkans, along with its abundant natural resources and youthful workforce, positions it as an attractive destination for investment and economic development.

One of the key drivers of Albania's economy is its vibrant tourism sector, which has experienced rapid growth in recent years. The country's stunning natural landscapes, rich cultural heritage, and Mediterranean coastline attract millions of tourists annually, contributing significantly to economic growth, job creation, and foreign exchange earnings.

In addition to tourism, Albania's economy is supported by other key sectors such as agriculture, energy, manufacturing, and services.

Agriculture remains an important contributor to the economy, employing a significant portion of the population and supplying domestic and international markets with a variety of products, including fruits, vegetables, and dairy.

The energy sector also plays a vital role in Albania's economy, with the country boasting abundant hydroelectric potential, making it a net exporter of electricity to neighboring countries. Investments in renewable energy sources, such as hydropower and solar, have further bolstered Albania's energy independence and sustainability.

Albania's manufacturing sector has seen growth in recent years, driven by investments in textiles, food processing, construction materials, and automotive components. The country's favorable labor costs, proximity to European markets, and improved business climate have attracted foreign investors seeking to establish production facilities and access regional markets.

Despite these opportunities, Albania's economy faces several challenges that hinder its full potential for growth and development. High levels of informal economic activity, corruption, inadequate infrastructure, and limited access to finance are among the key challenges facing Albania's economy. Additionally, the country's reliance on remittances from Albanians working abroad, particularly in Europe, exposes it to external shocks and economic vulnerabilities.

Furthermore, Albania's integration into the European Union remains a long-term goal, but challenges related to rule of law, governance, and economic competitiveness must be addressed to realize this ambition fully. The government is committed to implementing reforms to improve the business climate, enhance transparency, strengthen institutions, and promote inclusive growth.

In conclusion, Albania's economy is characterized by both opportunities and challenges, with the potential for continued growth and development supported by ongoing reforms, investments, and regional integration efforts. By addressing key challenges and leveraging its strengths, Albania can unlock its full economic potential and create opportunities for prosperity and well-being for its citizens.

Healthcare System in Albania: Past and Present

The healthcare system in Albania has undergone significant changes since the country's transition from communism in the early 1990s, transitioning from a centralized, state-controlled system to one that is more decentralized and market-oriented.

Historically, healthcare in Albania was characterized by a centralized, state-controlled system that provided universal access to healthcare services to all citizens free of charge. However, the collapse of communism and the subsequent economic and political transition led to significant challenges for the healthcare sector, including underfunding, shortages of medical supplies and equipment, and a decline in the quality of care.

Following the transition, Albania embarked on a series of reforms aimed at modernizing and strengthening its healthcare system to meet the needs of a changing society. These reforms included decentralization of healthcare delivery, privatization of healthcare facilities and services, and introduction of health insurance schemes to improve access and quality of care.

Today, Albania operates a mixed healthcare system that combines public and private providers, with the Ministry of Health overseeing policy development and regulation. The public healthcare system is funded through taxation and provides a basic package of healthcare services to all citizens, while the private sector offers additional services for those who can afford to pay.

Despite progress in healthcare reform, Albania's healthcare system continues to face numerous challenges. One of the major challenges is inadequate funding, with healthcare expenditure as a percentage of GDP remaining relatively low compared to other European countries. This has resulted in underinvestment in healthcare infrastructure, medical equipment, and human resources, leading to disparities in access and quality of care across different regions of the country.

Another challenge is the shortage of healthcare professionals, particularly doctors and nurses, due to emigration, low salaries, and poor working conditions. This shortage has resulted in overcrowded hospitals, long waiting times, and limited access to specialized care in some areas.

Additionally, healthcare in Albania is facing challenges related to quality and safety of care, including outdated medical equipment, lack of standardized protocols and guidelines, and inadequate monitoring and evaluation systems. These issues have raised concerns about patient safety and quality of care, prompting calls for further reforms and investments in healthcare infrastructure and services.

Despite these challenges, Albania has made progress in improving healthcare outcomes in recent years, with notable achievements in areas such as vaccination coverage, maternal and child health, and communicable disease control. The government has also launched initiatives to improve primary healthcare services, strengthen health promotion and disease prevention efforts, and enhance emergency medical services.

Looking ahead, Albania faces the ongoing challenge of balancing limited resources with the growing demand for healthcare services and the need to address emerging health threats such as noncommunicable diseases, antimicrobial resistance, and pandemics. By investing in healthcare infrastructure, strengthening primary care, and enhancing health workforce capacity, Albania can continue to improve access to quality healthcare and achieve better health outcomes for its population.

Transportation Infrastructure in Albania

Albania's transportation infrastructure plays a critical role in facilitating economic growth, trade, and mobility, connecting the country to regional and international markets and promoting social and economic development.

The road network forms the backbone of Albania's transportation system, accounting for the majority of passenger and freight movement within the country. Over the past two decades, significant investments have been made in upgrading and expanding Albania's road infrastructure, including the construction of new highways, bridges, and tunnels, as well as rehabilitation and maintenance of existing roads.

The construction of the Trans-European Transport Network (TEN-T) corridors, such as the Adriatic-Ionian Highway and the Pan-European Corridor VIII, has enhanced Albania's connectivity with neighboring countries and improved access to major ports and trade routes. These investments have reduced travel times, increased road safety, and stimulated economic activity in regions along the corridors.

Despite progress, challenges remain in Albania's road network, including the need for further investment in rural and secondary roads, addressing congestion and traffic bottlenecks in urban areas, and improving road safety measures to reduce accidents and fatalities. The government is committed to addressing these challenges through continued investments in road infrastructure and implementation of road safety initiatives.

In addition to roads, Albania also has a developing rail network that plays a vital role in transporting passengers and freight across the country. The railway network, operated by the Albanian Railways (HSH), connects major cities and ports, providing an alternative mode of transportation for passengers and goods. Investments in railway infrastructure and rolling stock are underway to modernize and expand the rail network, improve efficiency, and enhance connectivity with neighboring countries.

Albania's air transportation infrastructure consists of several international airports, including Tirana International Airport Nënë Tereza, which serves as the country's main gateway for air travel. The expansion and modernization of airport facilities, runway upgrades, and navigation equipment enhancements have increased airport capacity, improved service quality, and attracted new airlines and routes to Albania.

Maritime transportation is also vital to Albania's economy, with several major ports along the Adriatic and Ionian coasts serving as gateways for international trade and passenger traffic. Investments in port infrastructure, dredging, and logistics facilities have enhanced Albania's maritime connectivity and competitiveness, supporting trade and tourism development.

Looking ahead, Albania's transportation infrastructure will continue to evolve to meet the growing demands of a modern economy and society. Key priorities include further investments in road and rail infrastructure, integration with regional transport networks, promotion of sustainable and multimodal transportation solutions, and adoption of advanced technologies to improve efficiency and safety across all modes of transportation. By addressing these priorities, Albania can strengthen its position as a vital transportation hub in the Western Balkans and contribute to regional connectivity and economic integration.

Sports and Recreation in Albania

Sports and recreation play an integral role in promoting physical fitness, fostering social connections, and enhancing the overall well-being of individuals and communities across Albania. Football, or soccer, is the most popular sport in Albania, with a passionate fan base and a rich tradition of competitive play. The Albanian Superliga is the country's top professional football league, featuring clubs from across the country competing for the national championship. The national football team, known as the "Red and Blacks," has a storied history and competes in international tournaments such as the UEFA European Championship and FIFA World Cup.

In addition to football, basketball enjoys widespread popularity in Albania, with both amateur and professional leagues attracting players and fans of all ages. The Albanian Basketball League showcases local talent and provides opportunities for young athletes to develop their skills and compete at the national level. Basketball courts can be found in communities throughout Albania, serving as gathering places for friendly competition and recreational play.

Volleyball is another popular sport in Albania, with both indoor and beach volleyball attracting enthusiasts and competitive players alike. The Albanian Volleyball Federation oversees the development of the sport, organizing leagues, tournaments, and training programs to promote participation and excellence in volleyball at all levels. Beach volleyball tournaments held along Albania's stunning coastline draw athletes and spectators from around the country and beyond.

Wrestling holds a special place in Albanian culture, with a long history of traditional folk wrestling known as "Burek." This ancient sport emphasizes strength, skill, and agility, with wrestlers competing in various weight categories to demonstrate their prowess and earn respect within their communities. Burek tournaments and exhibitions showcase the athleticism and cultural heritage of Albanian wrestling traditions.

Other popular sports and recreational activities in Albania include athletics, swimming, cycling, hiking, and mountaineering, all of which take advantage of the country's diverse landscapes and natural beauty. Albania's rugged mountains, pristine lakes, and scenic coastlines offer endless opportunities for outdoor adventure and exploration, attracting outdoor enthusiasts and nature lovers from near and far.

The Albanian government, along with sports federations and community organizations, actively promotes participation in sports and recreational activities as part of a healthy and active lifestyle. Investments in sports facilities, infrastructure, and programs support grassroots development, talent identification, and elite athlete training, fostering a culture of sports excellence and achievement in Albania.

In conclusion, sports and recreation are integral components of Albanian society, providing opportunities for physical activity, social interaction, and personal growth. From football fields to basketball courts, from wrestling arenas to hiking trails, Albanians of all ages and backgrounds come together to pursue their passions, stay active, and enjoy the benefits of a vibrant sporting culture.

Prospects and Challenges for Albania in the 21st Century

As Albania continues its journey of development and transformation, it grapples with a myriad of opportunities and obstacles that will shape its future trajectory.

One of the key prospects for Albania in the 21st century lies in its aspirations for European integration. Since gaining candidate status for European Union (EU) membership in 2014, Albania has made significant strides in aligning its laws, institutions, and policies with EU standards and norms. Accession negotiations with the EU offer Albania the potential to deepen its economic ties, enhance political stability, and strengthen democratic governance. However, the path to EU membership is fraught with challenges, including the need for further reforms, addressing corruption and rule of law issues, and overcoming skepticism from some EU member states.

Another prospect for Albania is its strategic location in the Western Balkans region, which positions it as a key player in regional cooperation and integration efforts. Through initiatives such as the Berlin Process and the Western Balkans Six, Albania has the opportunity to foster closer ties with neighboring countries, promote economic cooperation, and address common challenges such as infrastructure development, energy security, and environmental sustainability. Regional cooperation also opens up new avenues for trade, investment, and cultural exchange, driving economic growth and prosperity in Albania and the wider region.

Albania's rich natural resources, including its stunning landscapes, biodiversity, and cultural heritage, present opportunities for sustainable development and tourism growth in the 21st century. With its pristine beaches, rugged mountains, and ancient historical sites, Albania has the potential to become a sought-after destination for ecotourism, adventure travel, and cultural tourism. Investments in infrastructure, hospitality, and environmental conservation are essential to capitalize on these opportunities and unlock the full potential of Albania's tourism sector.

However, Albania also faces significant challenges that threaten to impede its progress and development in the 21st century. Economic challenges, including high unemployment, low wages, and income inequality, remain persistent issues that require innovative solutions and targeted interventions to create jobs, stimulate growth, and reduce poverty. Structural reforms to improve the business climate, attract investment, and diversify the economy away from reliance on remittances and traditional sectors are essential for long-term economic sustainability.

Social challenges, such as demographic shifts, migration, and urbanization, pose additional complexities for Albania in the 21st century. Rapid population growth, coupled with emigration of skilled workers and brain drain, strain social services, infrastructure, and human capital development. Addressing these challenges requires comprehensive policies and programs to invest in education, healthcare, and social protection systems, as well as efforts to retain and attract talent, particularly among youth and the diaspora.

Furthermore, Albania faces environmental challenges, including pollution, deforestation, and climate change, which threaten its natural resources, ecosystems, and public health. Mitigating these challenges requires concerted efforts to promote sustainable development, conserve biodiversity, and transition to a low-carbon economy. Investments in renewable energy, green infrastructure, and environmental conservation are crucial for safeguarding Albania's natural heritage and ensuring a healthy and resilient future for its citizens.

In conclusion, Albania stands at a crossroads in the 21st century, with a range of prospects and challenges that will shape its trajectory in the years to come. By embracing opportunities for European integration, regional cooperation, tourism development, and sustainable growth, while addressing economic, social, and environmental challenges, Albania can chart a course towards a prosperous and resilient future for generations to come.

Epilogue

As we come to the end of this comprehensive exploration of Albania, it's fitting to reflect on the journey we've embarked upon together. Throughout this book, we've delved into the rich tapestry of Albania's history, culture, and landscape, uncovering its ancient roots, dynamic present, and promising future.

From the ancient civilizations of Illyria to the modern era of European integration, Albania has traversed a remarkable path of resilience, adaptation, and transformation. Its strategic location in the heart of the Balkans has shaped its destiny, influencing its interactions with neighboring cultures, empires, and ideologies over the centuries.

Albania's diverse cultural heritage, with influences from Illyrian, Roman, Byzantine, Ottoman, and European civilizations, is a testament to its enduring spirit of inclusivity, tolerance, and creativity. Its linguistic and religious diversity, alongside its traditions of hospitality, folk music, and folklore, reflect the mosaic of identities that define the Albanian people and their collective identity.

The natural beauty of Albania, from its rugged mountains to its pristine coastline, captivates the imagination and beckons adventurers and travelers to explore its hidden treasures. Its biodiversity, with endemic species and protected areas, underscores the importance of environmental conservation and sustainable development for future generations.

As Albania looks to the future, it faces both opportunities and challenges on the road ahead. The prospect of European integration offers the promise of greater prosperity, stability, and cooperation, while the need for economic reforms, social development, and environmental stewardship demands concerted efforts and visionary leadership.

In closing, Albania stands at a crossroads of history, poised to embrace the opportunities of the 21st century while preserving the timeless values and traditions that define its essence. As we bid farewell to this journey, may we carry with us the enduring lessons and inspirations of Albania, a land of contrasts, complexities, and endless possibilities.

Printed in Dunstable, United Kingdom